REVOLUTIONIZE YOUR WAREHOUSE

Embrace the Smart Technology That Will Transform Your Business

SOMIL NISHAR

CONTENTS

INTRODUCTION

In the ever-evolving landscape of modern business, the efficient management of warehouses has emerged as a pivotal factor in maintaining competitiveness and sustaining growth. Warehouses, once perceived as mere storage facilities, have now become strategic hubs in the supply chain because they influence the timely delivery of products, customer satisfaction, and overall business success. This transformation has been driven by a confluence of factors, including the rise of e-commerce, the globalization of markets, and the shifting expectations of consumers.

In this context, the emergence of smart technologies marks a revolutionary turning point in the way warehouses are operated and optimized. Smart technologies, which encompass a spectrum of innovations, such as the Internet of Things (IoT), Artificial Intelligence (AI), Big Data analytics, and automation, have the potential to transcend the traditional limitations of warehouse management. They empower businesses to collect, process, and leverage data in unprecedented ways while facilitating real-time decision-making, enhancing operational efficiency, and ultimately redefining the very essence of warehousing.

THE SIGNIFICANCE OF EFFICIENT WAREHOUSE MANAGEMENT

Efficient warehouse management holds the key to unlocking a series of benefits that extend far beyond the confines of the warehouse walls. With the increasing demand for rapid order fulfillment, accurate inventory tracking, and seamless supply chain integration, the stakes have never been higher. Businesses today are faced with the challenge of meeting these expectations while optimizing costs, streamlining processes, and ensuring a safe working environment for employees.

A well-managed warehouse contributes to reduced lead times, improved order accuracy, and enhanced customer satisfaction, thereby strengthening brand reputation and customer loyalty. Moreover, efficient warehouse operations mitigate the risk of overstocking or stockouts and enable companies to make informed decisions based on accurate inventory data. This, in turn, minimizes operational costs and enhances overall profitability.

THE EMERGENCE OF SMART TECHNOLOGIES

The digital era has ushered in a time of transformation across industries, and warehouses are no exception. Smart technologies have emerged as a formidable force that is capable of addressing the complexities and challenges inherent in modern warehouse management. The Internet of Things (IoT) facilitates the interconnectivity of devices and enables real-time monitoring and control of assets. Artificial Intelligence (AI) leverages data to make intelligent predictions and decisions and optimizes processes that were once driven by manual efforts. Big Data analytics provides insights into consumer behavior and market trends, which enables businesses to align their operations with changing demands. Automation and robotics have redefined material handling to minimize errors and improve operational efficiency.

THE BOOK'S GOAL: GUIDING BUSINESSES IN TRANSFORMATION

The goal of this book is to serve as a comprehensive guide for businesses that are seeking to embrace and harness the potential of smart technologies for warehouse transformation. It is designed to demystify the complexities of these technologies and provide actionable insights and practical strategies for their successful implementation. From understanding the foundational concepts to navigating the challenges of integration, this book offers a roadmap to revolutionizing warehouse operations.

Throughout the chapters that follow, we will delve into the specifics of IoT, AI, Big Data analytics, and automation while exploring their applications and highlighting real-world case studies that showcase their impact. We will address common concerns and challenges that businesses may encounter on their transformation journey and provide expert advice on change management and fostering a culture of innovation.

As you embark on this journey through the pages of

"Revolutionize Your Warehouse: Embrace the Smart Technology That Will Transform Your Business," you will gain the knowledge and insights needed to steer your business toward a future where your warehouse is not just a space for storage, but a dynamic hub that drives efficiency, customer satisfaction, and sustained growth.

CHAPTER 1

The Evolving Warehouse Landscape

Warehousing, once considered a mundane component of the supply chain, has undergone a remarkable evolution that has been driven by technological advancements, shifting consumer demands, and the rise of e-commerce. This chapter provides a comprehensive overview of the historical development of warehouse management, the challenges it has faced over time, and how external factors, like e-commerce, globalization, and changing consumer behavior, have fundamentally transformed warehouse operations. Additionally, this chapter introduces the concept of a "smart warehouse" and elucidates its transformative benefits.

HISTORICAL OVERVIEW OF WAREHOUSE MANAGEMENT AND ITS CHALLENGES

Warehouse management has a rich history that dates back to ancient civilizations when storehouses played a vital role in preserving and protecting valuable resources. However, it wasn't until the industrial revolution that the concept of organized warehouse management began to take shape. During this period, warehouses transformed from simple storage spaces to essential components of industrial supply chains.

Early warehouses were characterized by manual labor and limited technological advancements. Workers physically counted and recorded inventory, and goods were stored in a relatively haphazard manner. The primary function of these warehouses was to hold surplus stock for manufacturers and traders. Challenges of this era included inefficiency in inventory tracking, suboptimal use of space, and the lack of standardized processes.

As the 20th century progressed, warehouse management started to undergo systematic changes. The emergence of standardized inventory management systems, such as Just-in-Time (JIT) and Total Quality Management (TQM), aimed to optimize the flow of goods, reduce waste, and improve overall efficiency. Warehouses adopted these practices to varying degrees, but challenges, like inaccurate inventory counts, slow order processing, and inefficient storage methods, persisted.

The mid-20th century also witnessed the introduction of computerized systems, which began to replace manual record-keeping. This marked a significant step toward automation and enabled more accurate inventory tracking and faster data processing. However, these early computer systems were expensive and complex, which limited their adoption to larger businesses.

Globalization in the latter half of the 20th century introduced new challenges to warehouse management. As businesses expanded their operations across borders, warehouses had to contend with managing diverse inventories to cater to different markets, complying with varying regulations, and handling the complexities of international shipping.

The dawn of the 21st century brought about the digital age and the rapid rise of e-commerce. Online retail giants, like Amazon, disrupted traditional business models, which necessitated warehouses to adapt to a new reality. The shift from bulk orders to individual shipments posed challenges to warehouses designed for mass storage. The demand for faster order fulfillment, accurate inventory management, and real-time tracking became paramount.

Additionally, changing consumer behavior, influenced by the convenience of online shopping, led to higher expectations for the entire shopping experience. Consumers now demanded rapid delivery, easy returns, and transparent communication throughout the fulfillment process. Traditional warehouses were ill-prepared to handle these demands efficiently.

The historical evolution of warehouse management reflects a progression from basic storage facilities to complex and technologically driven hubs within the supply chain. Challenges, such as manual inventory management, inefficiency in space utilization, and slow order processing, have persisted throughout history. These challenges were amplified by globalization, e-commerce, and evolving consumer expectations. The subsequent chapters of this book will explore how smart technologies can address these challenges and revolutionize warehouse management in the modern era.

IMPACT OF E-COMMERCE, GLOBALIZATION, AND CHANGING CONSUMER BEHAVIOR

The dynamics of modern business have been profoundly influenced by three interconnected forces: e-commerce, globalization, and changing consumer behavior. These factors have collectively transformed the way goods are produced, distributed, and consumed, exerting a significant impact on warehouse operations and management.

1. E-commerce Revolution

The rise of e-commerce has redefined the retail landscape and fundamentally altered how consumers shop and how businesses operate. Online marketplaces and digital storefronts have enabled customers to purchase products from the comfort of their homes, thus driving a surge in demand for speedy and reliable order fulfillment.

Challenges for Warehouses: Traditional warehouses that were designed for bulk shipments struggled to adapt to the increasing volume of individual orders. The shift from pallets to parcels demanded new strategies for storage, picking, and packing.

Impact on Warehousing: Warehouses had to evolve to accommodate the higher frequency of smaller shipments. The need for efficient order picking, accurate inventory tracking, and streamlined returns management became critical.

2. Globalization and Supply Chain Complexity

Globalization has interconnected economies and markets across the world, which has led to complex supply chains that span continents. Businesses now source materials and products from diverse locations and are aiming to capitalize on cost efficiencies and access new markets.

Challenges for Warehouses: Managing inventory spread across multiple regions introduced challenges related to coordinating shipments, complying with varying regulations, and adapting to cultural nuances.

Impact on Warehousing: Warehouses had to develop strategies to handle diverse inventory, navigate complex international shipping and customs procedures, and synchronize operations across different time zones.

3. Changing Consumer Behavior

Consumers' expectations have shifted significantly due to the convenience and personalized experiences offered by digital commerce. Customers now demand rapid order fulfillment, transparency in tracking, and hassle-free returns.

Challenges for Warehouses: Fulfilling orders quickly and accurately became paramount. Warehouses faced pressure to provide real-time updates on order status and offer flexible return processes.

Impact on Warehousing: Warehouses had to restructure their processes to achieve faster order processing, implement technology for real-time tracking, and optimize reverse logistics for efficient returns handling.

These three forces—e-commerce, globalization, and changing consumer behavior—have converged to create a new paradigm for warehouse management. Traditional warehouses, which were designed for static inventory and bulk shipments, found themselves ill-equipped to meet the demands of this new landscape. Warehouses needed to re-invent themselves to become agile, efficient, and adaptable to meet the challenges posed by these transformative trends.

As a result, the concept of the "smart warehouse" emerged, and warehouses began leveraging technologies, like IoT, AI, Big Data, and automation to optimize process-es, enhance accuracy, and cater to the evolving demands of e-commerce, globalization, and consumer expectations. The subsequent chapters of this book will delve deeper into the specific technologies and strategies that enable warehouses to navigate and thrive in this complex and dynamic environ-ment.

INTRODUCTION TO THE CONCEPT OF A "SMART WAREHOUSE" AND ITS BENEFITS

In a world characterized by rapid technological advance-ments and evolving business dynamics, the concept of a "smart warehouse" has emerged as a beacon of innovation and efficiency. A smart warehouse represents a paradigm shift from traditional warehousing practices by integrating cutting-edge technologies to create a highly optimized, da-ta-driven ecosystem. Here, we introduce the concept of a smart warehouse and highlight its transformative benefits for modern businesses.

Defining a Smart Warehouse

At its core, a smart warehouse harnesses the power of

various technologies to enhance operational processes, improve decision-making, and elevate customer experiences. It leverages the Internet of Things (IoT), Artificial Intelligence (AI), Big Data analytics, and automation to create an interconnected environment where data flows seamlessly across devices, systems, and processes.

The Building Blocks

- **Internet of Things (IoT):** IoT involves embedding sensors and devices throughout the warehouse to collect real-time data on everything from inventory levels and equipment status to environmental conditions. This data is then transmitted and analyzed to facilitate informed decision-making.
- **Artificial Intelligence (AI):** AI empowers warehouses to analyze vast datasets, identify patterns, and make predictions. AI algorithms can optimize inventory management, predict demand fluctuations, and even automate decision-making processes.
- **Big Data Analytics:** Warehouses generate massive amounts of data daily. Big Data analytics processes this data to uncover insights, trends, and correlations that guide strategic decisions, enabling efficient inventory replenishment and demand forecasting.
- **Automation:** Automation involves the use of machines and robotics to perform tasks with

minimal human intervention. Automated processes streamline material handling, order picking, and packaging, which leads to reduced errors and enhanced speed.

Benefits of a Smart Warehouse

A smart warehouse that is powered by advanced technologies, such as the Internet of Things (IoT), Artificial Intelligence (AI), and automation, offers a wide range of benefits that significantly enhance warehouse operations, efficiency, and overall business performance. Here are some key benefits of a smart warehouse:

- **Improved Efficiency and Productivity:** Smart warehouses utilize automation, robotics, and AI-driven algorithms to streamline and optimize various tasks, such as inventory management, order picking, and packing. This leads to faster and more accurate operations, reduces the time and effort required to complete tasks, and increases overall productivity.
- **Real-time Visibility and Tracking:** IoT-enabled sensors and RFID technology provide real-time visibility into inventory levels, asset locations, and shipment status. This allows warehouse managers to track items throughout the supply chain, optimize inventory levels, and make informed decisions based on accurate data.
- **Optimized Inventory Management:** Smart

warehouses employ predictive analytics to forecast demand patterns and optimize inventory levels. This prevents overstocking and stockouts, reduces carrying costs, and ensures products are always available when needed.

- **Reduced Human Error:** Automation minimizes human involvement in repetitive and error-prone tasks and reduces the likelihood of errors, such as mis-picks and shipping mistakes. This results in improved order accuracy and customer satisfaction.
- **Faster Order Fulfillment:** Automated order picking and packing systems enable faster and more efficient order processing. This leads to shorter order-to-delivery cycles and quicker response times to customer orders.
- **Enhanced Safety:** Smart warehouses utilize robotics and automation to handle heavy or hazardous tasks, which reduces the risk of injuries to warehouse personnel. Advanced safety protocols, including collision avoidance systems, are integrated into robotic operations.
- **Optimized Space Utilization:** AI algorithms analyze warehouse layout and item dimensions to optimize storage and picking paths and maximize the utilization of available space. This reduces storage costs and ensures efficient use of the warehouse footprint.
- **Energy Efficiency:** Smart warehouses incor-

porate energy-efficient lighting, HVAC systems, and equipment. Sensors can detect occupancy and adjust lighting and climate control accordingly, which reduces energy consumption and costs.

- **Data-driven Insights:** AI and data analytics provide valuable insights into operational trends, performance metrics, and customer behaviors. These insights help warehouse managers make informed decisions to continuously improve processes.

- **Flexibility and Scalability:** Smart warehouses are designed with modularity and scalability in mind. This allows businesses to adapt to changing demands and easily expand their operations as needed.

- **Reduced Operational Costs:** Automation and optimization of processes lead to reduced labor costs, minimized waste, and lower operational expenses overall.

- **Enhanced Customer Satisfaction:** Faster order processing, accurate deliveries, and improved inventory availability directly contribute to higher levels of customer satisfaction. Customers receive their orders quickly and with minimal errors.

- **Compliance and Traceability:** IoT sensors and RFID technology enable better tracking of products, which is especially crucial for industries with stringent regulatory requirements. This improves traceability and aids in compliance with safety and quality standards.

- **Innovation and Competitive Advantage:** Implementing advanced technologies in the warehouse demonstrates a commitment to innovation. It gives companies a competitive edge by enabling them to offer faster and more efficient services compared to competitors with traditional warehouses.

The concept of a smart warehouse represents a strategic response to the challenges posed by e-commerce, globalization, and evolving consumer expectations. By leveraging the power of IoT, AI, Big Data analytics, and automation, businesses can unlock a multitude of benefits, ranging from enhanced efficiency and accuracy to improved customer experiences and cost savings. In the upcoming chapters, we will delve deeper into these technologies, their applications, and real-world success stories, and begin providing a comprehensive guide for businesses seeking to embrace the smart warehouse revolution.

CHAPTER 2

Building Blocks of a Smart Warehouse

In the dynamic landscape of modern warehouse management, the integration of cutting-edge technologies has given rise to the concept of a "smart warehouse." This chapter delves into the foundational technologies that constitute the building blocks of a smart warehouse: the Internet of Things (IoT), Artificial Intelligence (AI), Big Data, and Automation. By understanding the essence of these technologies and their collective potential, businesses can unlock unparalleled levels of operational efficiency, accuracy, and strategic insight.

UNDERSTANDING FOUNDATIONAL TECHNOLOGIES

Understanding foundational technologies is essential for comprehending the underlying principles that drive modern innovations and solutions. These technologies form the basis for various advancements and applications across industries. Here's an overview of some key foundational technologies:

- **Digitalization:** Digitalization involves converting analog information into digital formats that can be processed, stored, and transmitted by computers and other digital devices. It underpins the transformation of data, documents, and processes from physical to digital forms and enables easy access for sharing and analysis.

- **Computing:** Computing encompasses the principles and methods for processing information using computers. Central to computing is the concept of algorithms—step-by-step instructions for solving problems or performing tasks. These algorithms are executed by hardware components, including processors, memory, and storage devices.

- **Networking:** Networking involves the interconnection of devices and systems and enables communication and data exchange over distances. The Internet and local area networks (LANs) are prime examples of networking technologies. Networking protocols, such as TCP/IP, govern data transmission and ensure seamless connectivity.

- **Data Storage:** Data storage technologies encompass methods for storing and retrieving data. From traditional hard drives to solid-state drives (SSDs) and cloud storage solutions, these technologies determine how data is maintained and accessed over time.

- **Sensors and IoT:** Sensors are devices that capture real-world data, such as temperature, humidity, motion, and light. The Internet of

Things (IoT) leverages sensors and connectivity to collect, transmit, and analyze data from various physical objects, which enables smarter decision-making and automation.

- **Data Analytics:** Data analytics involves extracting insights from raw data using statistical techniques, machine learning, and artificial intelligence. It enables organizations to make informed decisions, predict trends, and discover patterns within large datasets.

- **Artificial Intelligence (AI):** AI refers to the simulation of human intelligence in machines. This encompasses technologies, like machine learning, natural language processing, and computer vision, that enable systems to learn from data, understand language, recognize patterns, and make decisions.

- **Machine Learning (ML):** Machine learning is a subset of AI that focuses on enabling systems to learn from data and improve their performance over time. ML algorithms identify patterns, make predictions, and automate tasks based on the data they've been trained on.

- **Robotics:** Robotics involves the design, creation, and operation of robots—autonomous or semi-autonomous machines that perform tasks with precision. It merges mechanical engineering with electronics, software, and AI, enabling robots to interact with and manipulate their environments.

- **Cloud Computing:** Cloud computing delivers computing services—including storage, processing power, and software—over the internet. It provides scalable and flexible resources that can be accessed on-demand and reduces the need for on-premises hardware and infrastructure.

- **Cybersecurity:** Cybersecurity technologies protect digital systems, networks, and data from unauthorized access, attacks, and threats. This includes methods like encryption, firewalls, intrusion detection systems, and secure coding practices.

- **Biotechnology:** Biotechnology involves the use of living organisms, cells, and biological systems to develop products and solutions. It includes areas like genetic engineering, bioinformatics, and medical biotechnology.

SYNERGIZING TECHNOLOGIES IN A SMART WAREHOUSE ECOSYSTEM

The concept of a smart warehouse revolves around the harmonious interaction and synergy of several key technologies: the Internet of Things (IoT), Artificial Intelligence (AI), Big Data analytics, and Automation. These technologies collectively create an ecosystem that redefines warehouse management and enables dynamic and data-driven operations. This section delves into how these technologies synergize to form a cohesive smart warehouse ecosystem.

Data Collection Through IoT

The foundation of the smart warehouse ecosystem is built on the Internet of Things. IoT devices, including sensors, RFID tags, and connected machinery, continuously collect data from various points within the warehouse. These devices monitor conditions, such as inventory levels, equipment health, environmental factors, and even employee movement. This real-time data collection creates a constant stream of information that serves as the raw material for further analysis and decision-making.

Big Data Analytics Unveiling Insights

The influx of data generated by IoT devices would be overwhelming without the analytical capabilities of Big Data. Big Data analytics platforms process and analyze vast datasets and identify patterns, trends, and anomalies that would be nearly impossible to detect through manual analysis. These insights provide valuable information about inventory turnover, demand fluctuations, seasonal trends, and operational inefficiencies.

AI-Driven Decision-Making

Artificial Intelligence takes the insights derived from Big Data analytics to the next level by transforming them into actionable decisions. AI algorithms recognize patterns that humans might overlook and enable predictive and prescriptive analysis. For instance, AI can forecast demand based on historical data, optimize inventory levels, and predict maintenance needs for equipment.

Automation for Real-time Action

Automation acts as the bridge between data analysis and real-world action. Automation systems use the insights and decisions generated by AI to orchestrate processes seamlessly. Robots and automated machinery execute tasks, such as order picking, sorting, and packaging, and follow optimized routes suggested by AI algorithms. This real-time execution minimizes human error and maximizes efficiency.

Feedback Loop and Continuous Improvement

The synergy in a smart warehouse ecosystem doesn't end with execution. The data collected during automation and operations are fed back into the system, which closes the loop and enables continuous improvement. This feedback enhances the accuracy of AI predictions, refines operational strategies, and contributes to a dynamic cycle of optimization.

Benefits of the Synergistic Ecosystem

- **Real-time Responsiveness:** The continuous flow of data, from IoT devices to AI-driven automation, enables warehouses to respond to changes in demand and conditions in real-time.
- **Enhanced Efficiency**: The synergy of technologies streamlines processes, reduces delays, and minimizes errors, resulting in higher operational efficiency.
- **Optimized Resource Allocation:** AI algorithms analyze data to allocate resources effec-

tively, whether it's labor, equipment, or inventory.

- **Improved Decision-Making:** The insights derived from Big Data and AI enable data-driven decision-making, which enhances accuracy and reduces guesswork.
- **Adaptability:** The integrated ecosystem allows warehouses to adapt to changing conditions, such as shifting demand patterns or unexpected disruptions.

The smart warehouse ecosystem demonstrates the power of integration and synergy among IoT, Big Data analytics, AI, and automation. By seamlessly connecting data collection, analysis, decision-making, and action, this ecosystem transforms traditional warehouses into agile, data-driven hubs of efficiency. In the following chapters, we'll explore each technology in more detail, while uncovering their applications and exploring real-world examples of their implementation in warehouses across industries.

REAL-LIFE EXAMPLES OF SUCCESSFUL IMPLEMENTATION

Numerous businesses across industries have embraced these technologies to reimagine their warehouse operations and achieve remarkable results:

- **Amazon:** The e-commerce giant's fulfillment centers exemplify the integration of IoT, AI, and automation. IoT sensors monitor inventory levels, AI algorithms optimize picking routes, and robots execute order fulfillment tasks, resulting in speedy and accurate deliveries.

- **DHL:** The global logistics company employs IoT-enabled tracking devices to monitor shipments' temperature and conditions in real-time. Big Data analytics process this information to ensure product quality and regulatory compliance.

- **Walmart:** The retail giant utilizes AI-powered demand forecasting to optimize inventory levels and anticipate customer preferences. This leads to efficient replenishment, reduced stockouts, and increased customer satisfaction.

These real-life examples underscore the potential of a smart warehouse to revolutionize traditional operations. By aligning IoT, AI, Big Data, and automation in a harmonious ecosystem, businesses can expect improved efficiency, reduced costs, enhanced customer experiences, and a competitive edge in a rapidly evolving market.

CHAPTER 3

IOT in Warehouse Management

The integration of the Internet of Things (IoT) technology has revolutionized the way warehouses operate and has ushered in a new era of data-driven and interconnected management. This chapter delves into the role of IoT in warehouse management and highlights its capacity to connect devices, assets, and systems to optimize various aspects of operations. We will explore how IoT enables real-time tracking, enhances inventory management, and even predicts maintenance needs. Through case studies, we will illustrate how IoT implementation has transformed inventory accuracy and led to significant operational cost reductions.

EXPLAINING IOT'S ROLE IN CONNECTIVITY

At the heart of IoT lies the ability to connect various devices, assets, and systems within the warehouse. This connectivity forms a digital nervous system that collects, transmits, and processes data in real-time. IoT-enabled sensors, RFID tags, and smart devices create a network that communicates data and allows for a comprehensive view of the warehouse's functioning.

The transformative power of the Internet of Things (IoT) in warehouse management lies in its ability to create a web of connectivity among devices, assets, and systems. This interconnected network forms the backbone of a smart warehouse and enables seamless data exchange, real-time monitoring, and informed decision-making. Let's delve into the intricate role of IoT in establishing connectivity within a warehouse ecosystem.

Sensor Deployment

IoT begins with the strategic deployment of sensors, RFID tags, and smart devices throughout the warehouse. These devices are strategically placed on assets, such as shelves, inventory items, equipment, and vehicles. Each device is equipped with the capability to collect and transmit data.

Data Collection

IoT-enabled devices continuously collect various types of data ranging from environmental factors, like temperature and humidity, to operational metrics, like movement, usage, and performance. This data forms a continuous stream of information that provides insights into the state and behavior of assets and processes within the warehouse.

Data Transmission

The collected data is transmitted via wireless networks to a central hub or cloud-based platform for processing and analysis. This enables real-time access to information regardless of location, which allows warehouse managers and personnel to make informed decisions based on current and accurate data.

Centralized Monitoring

In the central hub or cloud platform, data from various devices is aggregated and organized for easy monitoring and analysis. Warehouse managers can access a comprehensive overview of the warehouse's operations, asset status, and environmental conditions from a single dashboard.

Real-Time Insights

IoT provides real-time insights into various facets of warehouse management. For instance, sensors on inventory shelves can relay information about stock levels and movement and get instant updates on inventory status. Sensors on machinery can offer insights into equipment performance and identify potential issues before they escalate.

Interconnected Decision-Making

The interconnected data from IoT devices facilitates data-driven decision-making. Managers can identify patterns, trends, and anomalies that may go unnoticed through manual observation. This insight informs strategies for inventory optimization, demand forecasting, process improvement, and resource allocation.

Proactive Responses

IoT's real-time nature allows for proactive responses

to potential issues. For example, if a temperature-sensitive product's storage area exceeds optimal conditions, an alert is triggered, thus enabling immediate corrective action to prevent spoilage.

Integration with Other Technologies

The data collected through IoT can be integrated with other technologies, such as AI and Big Data analytics. This synergy amplifies the power of the data and offers more accurate predictions, informed decision-making, and automated processes.

IoT's role in connectivity goes beyond the mere collection of data. It forms the foundation of a dynamic ecosystem where devices, assets, and systems communicate seamlessly while providing real-time insights that empower efficient and strategic warehouse management. By enabling warehouse stakeholders to make informed decisions based on accurate, up-to-the-minute data, IoT transforms warehouses from traditional storage spaces into intelligent hubs of innovation and efficiency.

UTILIZING IOT FOR REAL-TIME TRACKING

In the realm of warehouse management, the Internet of Things (IoT) has emerged as a game-changer, particularly in its role of enabling real-time tracking. This capability has revolutionized the way warehouses operate by providing continuous insights into the movement and location of assets. IoT sensors affixed to goods, shelves, and vehicles facilitate ongoing updates and empower managers to make informed decisions and streamline operations. Let's explore how IoT's real-time tracking capability is transforming warehouse management.

- **IoT Sensors Enabling Real-Time Tracking:** IoT sensors play a pivotal role in real-time tracking within warehouses. These sensors are attached to various assets, ranging from individual inventory items to storage racks and delivery vehicles. Equipped with GPS, RFID, and other tracking technologies, these sensors collect and transmit data on the asset's whereabouts, movement patterns, and status.

- **Continuous Updates for Efficient Operations**: The heart of IoT's real-time tracking lies in its ability to provide continuous updates. As assets equipped with IoT sensors move throughout the warehouse, their locations are constantly relayed to a central hub or cloud-based platform. This real-time stream of data ensures that managers and personnel always have the latest information on the asset's whereabouts.

- **Optimizing Inventory Management:** Real-time tracking enhances inventory management by offering accurate visibility into stock levels and locations. Warehouse managers can instantly locate specific items, reducing the time spent searching for inventory. This translates to improved order fulfillment times and minimized delays.

- **Monitoring Shipment Progress:** IoT's real-time tracking extends beyond the warehouse's confines. It offers a comprehensive view of the entire supply chain by enabling managers to monitor the progress of shipments in transit. This data empowers proactive decision-making, such as rerouting shipments to avoid delays or addressing issues promptly.

- **Efficient Order Picking and Delivery:** Real-time tracking enhances order picking and delivery processes. As orders are processed, IoT sensors guide workers to the exact location of items, which optimizes pick paths and reduces order processing times. For deliveries, real-time tracking allows for accurate ETA calculations and informed customer communication.

- **Preventing Theft and Loss:** Real-time tracking acts as a deterrent against theft and loss. If an assct, such as a high-value inventory item, deviates from its designated path or leaves the premises, alerts can be triggered. This proactive approach prevents unauthorized movements and enhances security.

- **Case Study: Amazon's Fulfillment Centers:** Amazon's utilization of IoT for real-time tracking exemplifies its impact. IoT sensors track the movement of goods from arrival at the warehouse to shipment. This data enables Amazon to optimize processes, reduce delays, and enhance customer satisfaction through accurate delivery estimates.

ENHANCING INVENTORY MANAGEMENT

IoT offers a transformative approach to inventory management. Sensors placed on shelves and racks monitor stock levels and automatically trigger reorder requests when supplies run low. This ensures that stockouts are minimized and the replenishment process is efficient. Real-time visibility into inventory levels enables accurate demand forecasting and prevents overstocking, which leads to optimized stock levels.

Predictive Maintenance through IoT

IoT's impact goes beyond inventory management. It plays a pivotal role in predictive maintenance. IoT sensors placed on equipment and machinery collect data on performance metrics, temperature, and usage patterns. AI-driven analysis of this data allows for the prediction of maintenance needs before equipment failure occurs. This proactive approach minimizes downtime, reduces maintenance costs, and increases overall operational efficiency.

Case Studies: Transformation of Inventory Accuracy and Operational Costs

- **Walmart:** The retail giant implemented RFID technology across its stores and warehouses. This IoT-driven system improved inventory accuracy from 65% to 95% and resulted in better stock visibility, reduced stockouts, and increased sales.

- **Maersk Line:** The shipping company embedded IoT sensors in its containers to track location, temperature, humidity, and shock levels. This real-time data allowed Maersk to ensure that goods remained in optimal conditions during transit, resulting in reduced spoilage and increased customer satisfaction.
- **UPS**: The logistics giant introduced IoT sensors in its delivery trucks to monitor vehicle health and driver behavior. By analyzing this data, UPS optimized routes, reduced fuel consumption, and extended vehicle lifespans, which led to substantial cost savings.

IoT's integration into warehouse management has reshaped traditional practices. Through real-time tracking, enhanced inventory management, and predictive maintenance, IoT enhances efficiency, accuracy, and cost-effectiveness. By examining real-world cases, we see how IoT implementation has resulted in tangible benefits, including everything from increased inventory accuracy to reduced operational costs. As technology advances, the potential for IoT to further revolutionize warehouse management continues to expand. The following chapters will delve into the integration of AI, Big Data analytics, and automation and will further elevate the capabilities of the smart warehouse ecosystem.

CHAPTER 4

Harnessing the Power of Big Data

In the landscape of modern warehouse management, the significance of data has transcended mere information—it has become a strategic asset that fuels informed decision-making and drives operational excellence. This chapter delves into the pivotal role of Big Data in warehouse operations and spans data collection, storage, and analysis. We will explore how data analytics is leveraged for demand forecasting, trend analysis, and process optimization. Through real-world examples, we'll illustrate how companies harness the power of Big Data to make informed decisions, enhance customer satisfaction, and ultimately gain a competitive edge.

THE SIGNIFICANCE OF DATA COLLECTION, STORAGE, AND ANALYSIS

In the realm of modern warehouse management, the significance of data has evolved from being a mere byproduct of operations to becoming a strategic asset that drives informed decision-making and operational excellence. This section delves into the critical importance of data collection, storage, and analysis within the context of harnessing Big

Data in warehouse operations.

- **Data Collection:** A Foundation for Insights: At the heart of the Big Data paradigm lies the robust collection of data. Warehouses are dynamic hubs where numerous activities unfold and generate a wealth of information. Data is generated at every stage, from the movement of inventory items and the utilization of equipment to employee interactions and order processing. This data, often in the form of real-time streams, is the foundation upon which insights are built.

- **Vast Volumes of Warehouse Data:** Warehouse operations generate vast volumes of data daily. Inventory management involves the movement of goods in and out, with each movement leaving a data trail. Equipment and machinery performance is monitored through sensors that record parameters, like temperature, pressure, and usage patterns. Employee interactions with inventory and machinery further contribute to the data pool. Collectively, these diverse data points offer a comprehensive view of warehouse operations.

- **Data Storage and Accessibility:** To harness the potential of Big Data, the generated data needs to be stored in accessible and secure repositories. Centralized databases or cloud platforms provide the infrastructure for data storage. This enables authorized personnel to retrieve and analyze data from various sources coherently and efficiently. The accessibility of data is a crucial aspect that underpins its usability.

- **Transforming Data through Analysis**: While data collection and storage are crucial, the true value of Big Data emerges through analysis. Raw data, in its unprocessed state, might seem overwhelming or disconnected. However, the process of data analysis involves applying algorithms and techniques to extract meaningful insights. Through this process, patterns, correlations, and trends that might otherwise go unnoticed are revealed.

- **Actionable Insights Guiding Decisions:** The insights derived from data analysis hold immense potential to guide strategic decisions. Warehouse managers can identify bottlenecks, optimize processes, and fine-tune resource allocation based on data-driven insights. For instance, analysis might reveal peak demand periods, thus creating opportunities for proactive staffing and inventory adjustments that cater to customer needs.

- **Revealing Hidden Patterns:** Beyond informing immediate decisions, data analysis can unveil hidden patterns that offer a deeper understanding of operations. These patterns might relate to seasonal demand trends, unusual equipment behaviors, or correlations between seemingly unrelated variables. Such insights can spark innovations, process improvements, and even new business models.

IMPLEMENTING DATA ANALYTICS FOR WAREHOUSE OPTIMIZATION

- **Demand Forecasting:** Big Data analytics enables accurate demand forecasting by analyzing historical sales data, seasonality trends, and external factors. This helps warehouses anticipate demand fluctuations, optimize inventory levels, and prevent stockouts or overstocking.
- **Trend Analysis:** Analyzing historical data reveals long-term trends in consumer preferences, which enables warehouses to adjust their inventory mix and stocking strategies accordingly. Trend analysis helps businesses stay ahead of changing market dynamics.
- **Process Optimization:** Big Data insights facilitate the identification of inefficiencies within warehouse processes. By analyzing data on order processing times, pick rates, and equipment utilization, warehouses can streamline operations, reduce bottlenecks, and enhance overall efficiency.

EXAMPLES OF COMPANIES LEVERAGING BIG DATA

- **Zara:** The fast-fashion retailer utilizes Big Data

analytics to track fashion trends in real-time. Data from social media, fashion blogs, and online searches are analyzed to anticipate upcoming trends. This data-driven approach allows Zara to adapt its inventory and product offerings rapidly.

- **FedEx**: The logistics giant employs Big Data analytics to optimize delivery routes and schedules. By analyzing factors like traffic patterns, weather conditions, and historical data, FedEx minimizes delivery delays and enhances customer satisfaction.

- **L.L.Bean:** The outdoor retailer uses Big Data to forecast demand for its products, particularly in relation to weather conditions. By analyzing historical sales data alongside weather forecasts, L.L.Bean ensures that the right products are available when customers need them.

ENHANCING CUSTOMER SATISFACTION

Leveraging Big Data enables warehouses to enhance customer satisfaction through improved order accuracy, faster fulfillment, and personalized experiences. Accurate demand forecasting and optimized inventory levels lead to better product availability, reduced backorders, and faster order processing. Data-driven insights also facilitate personalized recommendations and offer that can heighten customer engagement.

The strategic integration of Big Data into warehouse operations marks a transformative shift. Data collection, storage, and analysis pave the way for informed decision-making, process optimization, and enhanced customer satisfaction. By examining real-world examples of companies successfully leveraging Big Data, we see how data-driven insights lead to competitive advantages. As businesses continue to evolve, the power of Big Data remains a critical tool for navigating the complexities of the modern warehouse landscape.

CHAPTER 5

Artificial Intelligence and Machine Learning

In the landscape of modern warehouse management, Artificial Intelligence (AI) and Machine Learning (ML) have emerged as transformative forces that have reshaped traditional practices and propelled operational efficiency to new heights. This chapter delves into the realm of AI and ML within warehouse contexts and seeks to demystify their applications and illustrate how they revolutionize various facets of operations. From optimizing routes to enhancing order picking, detecting anomalies, and managing risks, AI-driven insights are redefining how warehouses operate.

DEMYSTIFYING AI AND MACHINE LEARNING

AI is the science of enabling machines to mimic human cognitive functions, such as learning, reasoning, and problem-solving. Machine Learning, a subset of AI, involves training machines to learn from data and improve their performance over time. In warehouse management, AI and ML leverage data to make predictions, optimize processes, and identify patterns that human operators might overlook.

In the dynamic landscape of warehouse management,

the terms "Artificial Intelligence" (AI) and "Machine Learning" (ML) have garnered attention as transformative technologies. Understanding their roles within warehouse contexts is essential to harnessing their potential for optimizing operations and driving efficiency. This section delves into the core concepts of AI and ML and breaks down their applications and benefits within warehouses.

Artificial Intelligence (AI) Defined

At its core, AI refers to the capability of machines to simulate human intelligence and decision-making processes. It enables machines to perform tasks that typically require human intelligence, such as learning from experience, recognizing patterns, making decisions, and solving problems.

Machine Learning (ML) Unveiled

Machine Learning, a subset of AI, focuses on the development of algorithms and models that enable computers to improve their performance on a specific task through learning from data. In other words, ML allows machines to learn and adapt based on experience that iteratively refines their capabilities without explicit programming.

AI AND ML IN WAREHOUSE CONTEXTS

In the world of warehouse management, AI and ML hold immense potential to revolutionize operations:

- **Demand Forecasting:** AI and ML algorithms analyze historical sales data, seasonal trends, and external factors to predict future demand accurately. This aids warehouses in optimizing inventory levels and preventing stockouts or overstocking.

- **Route Optimization:** AI analyzes data from various sources, including traffic patterns and delivery destinations, to optimize delivery routes. ML algorithms learn from historical route data, enabling better decision-making for efficient deliveries.

- **Anomaly Detection:** AI-driven systems monitor vast streams of data from sensors and equipment and identify anomalies that deviate from normal patterns. This allows warehouses to detect potential malfunctions or irregularities early, which leads to preventive maintenance and reduced downtime.

- **Order Picking Efficiency:** ML models learn from historical order-picking data to recommend the most efficient sequence for picking items. This reduces travel time, enhances order processing speed, and minimizes errors.

- **Process Optimization:** AI analyzes data on various warehouse processes to identify bottlenecks and inefficiencies. By recognizing patterns and correlations in the data, AI can suggest process improvements for enhanced efficiency.

BENEFITS OF DEMYSTIFYING AI AND ML

Enhanced Understanding

AI and ML are often seen as mysterious and complicated topics that cause confusion and skepticism among those who are not familiar with the technical intricacies. By demystifying these technologies, people gain a clearer understanding of what AI and ML entail, how they function, and what their potential applications are. This understanding can lead to more informed discussions and decisions about their implementation.

Informed Decision-Making

When individuals, including business leaders and policymakers, have a better grasp of AI and ML concepts, they can make more informed decisions about whether to adopt these technologies in their organizations or initiatives. They can evaluate the potential benefits and risks more accurately and make choices aligned with their goals.

Wider Adoption

Demystifying AI and ML can break down barriers to adoption. People are more likely to embrace technologies they understand. By presenting these technologies in simpler terms, you encourage a wider range of individuals to explore their applications and consider integrating them into their processes, products, or services.

Reduced Fear and Resistance

There's often fear and resistance associated with AI and automation due to concerns about job displacement and loss of control. Demystifying these technologies can help alleviate these fears by providing a more realistic perspective on how AI and ML can complement human capabilities and enhance various aspects of work and life rather than replacing humans outright.

Effective Communication

Clear communication is vital when discussing AI and ML projects with stakeholders, employees, and customers. Demystifying these technologies enables you to articulate their benefits, limitations, and potential impacts in a language that resonates with different audiences. This promotes better understanding and cooperation among all parties involved.

Stimulated Innovation

When AI and ML are demystified, more people, including non-technical individuals, can contribute innovative ideas and solutions that leverage these technologies. A broader understanding of AI and ML can lead to creative applications that might not have been considered within a narrow technical context.

Ethical Consideration

Demystifying AI and ML helps individuals recognize the ethical considerations associated with these technologies. With a better understanding of how decisions are made and data is processed, people are more likely to engage in discussions about fairness, bias, transparency, and accountability, which are critical aspects of responsible AI development and deployment.

Collaboration and Multidisciplinary Approaches

AI and ML projects often require collaboration between experts from various fields, including domain experts who might not have deep technical knowledge. Demystifying these technologies facilitates smoother interdisciplinary collaboration as professionals from diverse backgrounds can engage in meaningful discussions and contribute their expertise.

Education and Skill Development

By presenting AI and ML concepts in a more approachable manner, you encourage individuals to learn about these technologies. This can spark interest in pursuing educational opportunities related to AI and ML, which leads to a more skilled workforce capable of leveraging these technologies effectively.

APPLICATIONS OF AI IN WAREHOUSES

- **Route Optimization:** AI analyzes historical data on order volumes, traffic patterns, and delivery destinations to optimize delivery routes. This ensures efficient routing, reduces fuel consumption and delivery times, and ultimately leads to cost savings and improved customer satisfaction.

- **Order Picking Optimization:** AI optimizes order picking by determining the most efficient sequence for retrieving items from storage. It considers factors like order volume, item locations, and picker efficiency to reduce travel time and increase order processing speed.
- **Anomaly Detection**: AI systems continuously monitor data from sensors and equipment and detect anomalies that indicate potential malfunctions or deviations from normal operations. Early detection allows for preventive maintenance, which minimizes downtime and reduces operational disruptions.
- **Risk Management**: AI analyzes historical and real-time data to identify potential risks, such as stockouts, supply chain disruptions, or quality issues. This proactive approach enables warehouse managers to mitigate risks and respond swiftly to changing conditions.
- **Improved Decision-Making:** AI-driven insights provide warehouse managers with data-driven decision-making capabilities. By analyzing complex data sets, AI can suggest optimal stocking levels, suggest process improvements, and allocate resources effectively.
- **Reduced Errors**: Machine Learning algorithms minimize errors by learning from historical data. This is particularly relevant in order picking, where AI can recommend the best pick

path, reducing the likelihood of mistakes.

- **Real-time Adaptability:** AI's ability to process real-time data enables warehouses to swiftly adapt to changing conditions. For example, if an unexpected surge in demand occurs, AI can adjust staffing levels and inventory allocations in real-time.

- **Continuous Learning:** ML models learn and improve over time as they encounter new data. This iterative process enhances the accuracy of predictions and recommendations, which leads to increasingly optimized operations.

AI and Machine Learning represent the cutting edge of warehouse management innovation. By leveraging data-driven insights and predictive capabilities, warehouses can optimize routes, enhance order processing, detect anomalies, and manage risks. These technologies not only improve efficiency but also reduce errors and provide a competitive edge in an ever-evolving market. As AI continues to evolve, its transformative impact on warehouse operations is bound to expand and open new avenues for innovation and growth.

CHAPTER 6

Automation and Robotics

In the evolution of warehouse management, the integration of automation and robotics has emerged as a transformative force that is redefining traditional practices and reshaping the way operations are conducted. This chapter delves into the world of automation and robotics within warehouses while exploring the diverse forms they take and the profound impact they have on efficiency, productivity, and safety. From robotic process automation (RPA) to the deployment of autonomous drones, we'll delve into the intricacies of automation, its role in material handling and order fulfillment, and how real-world examples highlight its profound effects on labor efficiency and workplace safety.

EXPLORING VARIOUS FORMS OF AUTOMATION

Automation encompasses a wide spectrum of technologies that each contribute to the streamlining of warehouse processes:

- **Robotic Process Automation (RPA):** RPA involves the automation of rule-based tasks using software robots. These robots mimic human interactions with digital systems and perform tasks, like data entry, order processing, and inventory tracking with precision and speed.

- **Autonomous Drones:** Drones equipped with advanced sensors and navigation systems can autonomously scan shelves, track inventory, and even aid in order picking and item retrieval. They enhance efficiency by swiftly covering large areas and providing real-time data.

- **Robotic Material Handling:** Robots are deployed to handle the movement of goods within the warehouse. Automated guided vehicles (AGVs) and autonomous mobile robots (AMRs) can transport goods while reducing the need for manual labor in material movement.

THE ROLE OF ROBOTICS IN WAREHOUSE TASKS

- **Material Handling**: Robots excel in lifting, transporting, and organizing goods. They navigate the warehouse with precision, minimize the risk of damage, and optimize the use of available space.

- **Order Fulfillment:** Robots are adept at automating order picking and can help reduce the time it takes to retrieve items and fulfill customer orders. They follow optimized paths to efficiently gather items for shipping.

- **Repetitive Tasks:** Robots excel in tasks that require precision and repetition, such as packing items, sorting goods, and labeling packages. By taking over such tasks, robots free up human workers for more complex and value-added activities.

REAL-WORLD CASES HIGHLIGHTING THE IMPACT OF AUTOMATION

- **ASOS:** The online fashion retailer ASOS employs robotic automation for order fulfillment. Robots navigate the warehouse shelves, pick the ordered items, and transport them to packing stations. This system has significantly reduced order processing time and improved accuracy.
- **Ocado:** The online grocery retailer Ocado utilizes a combination of robots and automated systems to manage its warehouse operations. Robots work collaboratively to pick, pack, and sort groceries, which results in efficient order processing and minimal errors.
- **JD.com:** The Chinese e-commerce giant JD.com uses autonomous drones and delivery robots to transport packages between distribution centers and customers. This approach reduces delivery times and expands the reach of their services.

IMPACT ON LABOR EFFICIENCY AND SAFETY

The integration of automation and robotics within warehouse operations has far-reaching implications for labor efficiency and workplace safety. These technologies have the potential to transform how work is conducted, and can lead to increased productivity, streamlined processes, and improved safety measures. This section delves into the profound effects that automation and robotics have on these crucial aspects of warehouse management.

1. Enhancing Labor Efficiency

- **Repetitive and Monotonous Tasks**: Automation excels at taking over tasks that are repetitive and monotonous. These tasks, which can be mentally and physically draining for human workers, are efficiently handled by robots and automated systems. This allows human employees to focus on tasks that require critical thinking, problem-solving, and creativity.

- **Speed and Accuracy:** Robots equipped with advanced algorithms and sensors can perform tasks with unmatched speed and precision. This translates to faster order fulfillment, accurate inventory management, and reduced processing times. Automated systems consistently perform tasks without fatigue or distractions while ensuring a high level of accuracy.

- **Process Optimization:** Automation and robotics enable warehouses to optimize processes by eliminating bottlenecks and inefficiencies. Robots follow optimized paths for order picking, which minimizes travel time and ensures optimal use of warehouse space. This streamlining of processes enhances overall operational efficiency.

- **Scalability:** Automation allows warehouses to scale their operations easily. As order volumes increase, robots can be deployed to handle the additional workload without the need for extensive training or hiring processes. This scalability ensures that the warehouse can meet demand without compromising efficiency.

2. Improving Workplace Safety

- **Hazardous Tasks:** Automation and robotics are particularly valuable in handling tasks that pose risks to human workers. Tasks involving heavy lifting, working in confined spaces, or exposure to hazardous materials can be delegated to robots, which can prevent the risk of injuries and accidents.

- **Ergonomics and Health:** Automation minimizes the physical strain on human workers by handling tasks that require repetitive motions or strenuous effort. This reduces the risk of musculoskeletal injuries, promotes better ergonomics in the workplace, and contributes to the overall health and well-being of employees.

- **Risky Environments:** Automated systems are well-suited to work in environments that are hazardous to human workers, such as extreme temperatures, toxic fumes, or high altitudes. Robots can navigate these conditions without endangering human health.

- **Prevention of Accidents:** Automation reduces the occurrence of accidents caused by human error. Robots follow programmed paths and safety protocols that minimize the likelihood of collisions and mistakes that can lead to accidents.

The impact of automation and robotics on labor efficiency and safety is profound. By delegating repetitive tasks to machines and optimizing processes, warehouses enhance efficiency, accuracy, and productivity. Moreover, automation contributes to a safer work environment by handling tasks that pose risks to human workers and minimizing the occurrence of accidents. As warehouses continue to embrace automation, the potential for improved labor conditions and enhanced safety measures becomes increasingly evident and paves the way for a future of optimized operations and protected workforces.

Automation and robotics represent a significant leap forward in warehouse management. From RPA to robotic material handling, these technologies optimize processes, improve efficiency, and enhance safety. By embracing automation's potential and learning from real-world examples, warehouses can reap the benefits of streamlined operations and a safer work environment. As the field of automation continues to evolve, the possibilities for further innovation and optimization are limitless.

CHAPTER 7

Transforming the Fulfillment Process

In the realm of warehouse management, the evolution from traditional fulfillment approaches to smart, customer-centric strategies marks a paradigm shift that has revolutionized how products reach the hands of consumers. This chapter delves into the transformative journey of fulfillment and explores the progression from conventional methods to innovative and technology-driven approaches. We'll delve into the utilization of cutting-edge technology to offer diverse fulfillment options, including same-day delivery and click-and-collect services. Through real-world success stories, we'll illustrate how companies have elevated their customer experience by embracing advanced fulfillment strategies.

THE JOURNEY TO SMART, CUSTOMER-CENTRIC FULFILLMENT

The evolution of the fulfillment process from traditional methods to smart, customer-centric strategies marks a significant shift in the way warehouses operate and how products are delivered to consumers. This transformation is driven by technological advancements and changes in consumer expectations, which make it imperative to provide seamless and efficient experiences. Let's delve into the stages of this journey and how it has reshaped the warehouse landscape.

The fulfillment process has undergone a profound transformation and has evolved from the traditional warehousing and shipping approach to one that prioritizes customer satisfaction and operational efficiency:

- **Traditional Fulfillment:** In the past, warehouses primarily functioned as storage and distribution centers. Orders were processed manually, inventory was managed through basic systems, and shipping times were often inconsistent. The focus was on product availability and moving goods from the warehouse to the customer.

- **Technological Infusion:** As technology advanced, warehouses began incorporating automation, data analytics, and digital communication systems. Basic inventory management systems were replaced with more sophisticated software, which now allows for better tracking and management of goods. This laid the foundation for more efficient processes.

- **Customer-Centric Approach:** The shift towards customer-centric fulfillment was driven by changing consumer behavior and expectations. Customers began to demand faster delivery times, flexible options, and a seamless shopping experience. Warehouses responded by adopting technology to optimize processes and enhance customer satisfaction.

- **Smart Fulfillment Centers:** Modern warehouses evolved into smart fulfillment centers where technology plays a central role in every step of the process. Data-driven insights, automation, and real-time tracking capabilities are integrated into operations to streamline processes and improve efficiency.

- **Diverse Fulfillment Options:** In the journey to customer-centricity, warehouses diversified their fulfillment options to cater to different consumer needs. Same-day delivery, next-day delivery, click-and-collect, and micro-fulfillment centers emerged as solutions to offer convenience and flexibility.

- **Seamless Online-to-Offline Integration:** Click-and-collect services seamlessly bridge the gap between online and offline shopping. Customers can browse and order products online and then collect them from a physical store all while enjoying the convenience of both worlds.

- **Data-Driven Personalization:** One of the hallmarks of customer-centric fulfillment is the use of customer data to tailor experiences. Warehouses analyze buying patterns, preferences, and behaviors to offer personalized recommendations, promotions, and offers.

- **Enhanced Visibility and Transparency:** Technology enables real-time tracking of orders that provides customers with visibility into the status and location of their purchases. This transparency builds trust and reduces uncertainty, enhancing the overall experience.

- **Operational Efficiency:** Automation, robotics, and AI-driven insights optimize warehouse processes, resulting in higher efficiency and accuracy. Faster order processing, reduced errors, and optimized inventory management contribute to operational excellence.

- **Elevated Customer Satisfaction:** The culmination of this journey is elevated customer satisfaction. Customers experience fast, accurate, and convenient order fulfillment, leading to a positive perception of the brand and increased loyalty.

UTILIZING TECHNOLOGY FOR DIVERSE FULFILLMENT OPTIONS

- **Same-Day Delivery**: Advances in automation, real-time tracking, and route optimization have made same-day delivery feasible. Warehouses use AI and robotics to process and fulfill orders rapidly, which provides customers with almost instant gratification.

- **Click-and-Collect:** Technology enables click-and-collect services where customers order online and collect their purchases from a physical store. This seamless integration of online and offline channels enhances convenience for consumers.

- **Micro-Fulfillment Centers:** These compact fulfillment centers, which are located closer to urban areas, enable faster deliveries and efficient order processing. Automation and robotics play a crucial role in optimizing these micro-fulfillment operations.
- **Data-Driven Personalization:** By analyzing customer data, warehouses tailor their fulfillment strategies to individual preferences. Personalized recommendations, targeted promotions, and order history insights enhance the overall customer experience.

SUCCESS STORIES OF ADVANCED FULFILLMENT STRATEGIES

In the dynamic landscape of modern warehouse management, several companies have risen to prominence by successfully implementing advanced fulfillment strategies that optimize operations, enhance customer experiences, and elevate their competitive advantage. These success stories exemplify the transformative impact of embracing technology-driven approaches to fulfillment. Here are a few notable examples:

Amazon Prime

Strategy: Amazon Prime, a subscription-based service, offers members expedited shipping, including same-day and next-day delivery, on a wide range of products.

Impact: Amazon Prime has revolutionized customer expectations for delivery speed and convenience. By deploying massive fulfillment centers, utilizing robotics, and leveraging data analytics, Amazon Prime provides seamless and rapid order fulfillment. The service has attracted millions of subscribers and played a pivotal role in solidifying Amazon's position as an e-commerce giant.

Walmart's Micro-Fulfillment Centers

Strategy: Walmart has embraced micro-fulfillment centers, which are smaller warehouses located in urban areas, to optimize order processing and delivery times.

Impact: By decentralizing fulfillment centers, Walmart ensures that products are closer to customers so that delivery times are reduced and order processing is completed efficiently. Automation and robotics within these micro-fulfillment centers enhance accuracy and speed. This approach has strengthened Walmart's position as a competitive force in the online retail market.

Target's Drive Up Service

Strategy: Target introduced the "Drive Up" service that gives customers the option to order products online and have them brought to their cars in the store parking lot.

Impact: This strategy seamlessly combines online and offline experiences and offers customers the convenience of online shopping without the wait for shipping. It leverages real-time inventory data and location-based technology to orchestrate a smooth and efficient curbside pickup process. This innovative service has earned Target loyal customers and increased foot traffic to its physical stores.

Domino's Pizza

Strategy: Domino's Pizza pioneered the "Domino's AnyWare" initiative where customers place orders via various platforms, including social media, smart speakers, and even smart TVs.

Impact: By diversifying order channels, Domino's Pizza made ordering more accessible and convenient for customers. This omnichannel approach capitalizes on the platforms customers use daily and makes pizza orders quick and seamless. The initiative showcases how a focus on convenient fulfillment methods can enhance customer engagement and loyalty.

Jd.com's Drone Delivery

Strategy: JD.com, a major Chinese e-commerce company, has leveraged autonomous drones for last-mile delivery in remote areas.

Impact: By using drones for delivery, JD.com has overcome geographical challenges to provide access to customers who were previously underserved. This innovation not only showcases the potential of technology in expanding market reach but also demonstrates how advanced fulfillment strategies can redefine delivery norms.

ELEVATING CUSTOMER EXPERIENCE THROUGH ADVANCED FULFILLMENT

The integration of advanced fulfillment strategies within warehouse operations isn't just about optimizing processes—it's also about enhancing the overall customer experience. By leveraging technology-driven approaches, warehouses can offer a range of benefits that elevate customer satisfaction, loyalty, and engagement. This section delves into how advanced fulfillment strategies contribute to an elevated customer experience.

- **Convenience and Flexibility:** Advanced fulfillment strategies cater to the diverse preferences of modern consumers and offer them convenience and flexibility in how they receive their orders. Whether it's same-day delivery, click-and-collect, or micro-fulfillment centers, these options empower customers to choose the method that best aligns with their schedules and preferences.

- **Speed and Rapid Gratification**: In today's fast-paced world, customers appreciate prompt delivery. Advanced fulfillment technologies, such as same-day delivery enabled by robotics and efficient order processing, provide the rapid gratification that customers seek. This speed not only meets their immediate needs but also enhances their perception of the brand's responsiveness.

- **Personalization and Tailored Experiences:** Data-driven insights play a pivotal role in advanced fulfillment strategies. By analyzing customer data, warehouses can personalize recommendations, promotions, and offers based on individual preferences and buying behavior. This tailored approach creates a sense of being understood and valued and fosters a deeper connection with the brand.

- **Seamless Online-to-Offline Integration:** Click-and-collect services seamlessly bridge the gap between online and offline shopping experiences. Customers can enjoy the convenience of shopping from home while still having the option to physically collect their purchases. This integration enhances the overall shopping journey and empowers customers to choose the experience that suits them best.

- **Enhanced Transparency and Communication:** Technology-driven fulfillment often comes with real-time tracking capabilities. Customers can track the progress of their orders from the moment they're placed to the moment they're delivered. This transparency instills confidence in the process and reduces anxiety related to delivery times.

- **Competitive Differentiation:** Brands that offer advanced fulfillment strategies set themselves apart from competitors. When customers experience efficient and convenient order fulfillment, they're more likely to remember and choose that brand for future purchases. This competitive differentiation contributes to brand loyalty and long-term customer relationships.

- **Reduced Friction and Hassle:** Advanced fulfillment minimizes the friction and hassle associated with traditional shopping experiences. Waiting in long lines, dealing with out-of-stock items, and uncertain delivery times are challenges that these strategies aim to overcome. By removing these pain points, customers are left with a positive and smooth purchasing journey.
- **Enhanced Word-of-Mouth and Advocacy:** Satisfied customers are more likely to share their positive experiences with friends, family, and on social media. The convenience and efficiency of advanced fulfillment strategies can lead to organic word-of-mouth promotion and expand a brand's reach while attracting new customers.

The journey from traditional fulfillment to smart, customer-centric approaches has reshaped the warehouse landscape. Technology-driven options like same-day delivery, click-and-collect, and micro-fulfillment centers have transformed customer experiences and elevated operational efficiency. Real-world success stories demonstrate the impact of these strategies on customer satisfaction and business success. As warehouses continue to harness technology to reimagine fulfillment, the potential for further innovation and improved customer engagement remains boundless.

CHAPTER 8

Overcoming Challenges and Implementation Roadmap

As warehouses embark on the journey to embrace smart technology for transformation, they encounter a range of challenges that need to be addressed. From financial considerations to the integration of new systems and concerns about the existing workforce, navigating these obstacles requires a well-thought-out implementation roadmap. This chapter delves into the common challenges faced during the adoption of smart technology, provides a step-by-step guide to implementation, and offers expert advice on change management and fostering a culture of innovation.

ADDRESSING COMMON CHALLENGES

- **Cost Considerations:** Implementing smart technology can come with upfront costs for technology acquisition, infrastructure upgrades, and training. Balancing these expenses against potential long-term benefits is a challenge.

- **Integration Complexities:** Integrating new technology with existing systems can be complex and requires meticulous planning to ensure seamless operations.

- **Workforce Concerns**: Employees may fear job displacement due to automation or struggle to adapt to new technology, which can lead to resistance and decreased morale.

CREATING AN IMPLEMENTATION ROADMAP

Assessment and Planning:
- Conduct a comprehensive assessment of current operations and identify pain points and areas for improvement.
- Define clear goals and objectives for implementing smart technology that are aligned with the organization's strategic vision.

Technology Selection:
- Identify technologies that align with your warehouse's needs and goals and consider scalability and compatibility.
- Evaluate potential vendors and solutions based on their track record, support, and integration capabilities.

Pilot Testing:
- Begin with a pilot project to test the selected technology on a smaller scale.
- Gather feedback, address any issues, and fine-tune the implementation approach based on the

pilot's results.

Integration and Training:
- Ensure the new technology integrates seamlessly with existing systems to avoid disruptions.
- Provide comprehensive training to employees. Focusing on both technical skills and change management.

Change Management:
- Communicate the benefits of the new technology to employees. Addressing concerns and emphasizing the value it brings.
- Involve employees in the decision-making process and solicit their input to increase buy-in.

Scalable Rollout:
- Gradually implement the technology on a larger scale while monitoring performance and making necessary adjustments.

EXPERT ADVICE ON CHANGE MANAGEMENT

Change management plays a pivotal role in the successful adoption of smart technology within warehouse operations. As warehouses transition to embrace new technologies, navigating the human element of change is essential. Expert advice on change management provides valuable insights into how to guide employees through the process, foster buy-in, and ensure a smooth transition. Here are key pieces of advice from experts in the field:

- **Leadership Involvement:** Effective change begins at the top. Leaders must actively champion and support the adoption of new technology. Their visible commitment sends a clear message to employees that the change is endorsed and valued by the organization.

- **Open Communication:** Transparent and on-going communication is critical. Keep employees informed about the reasons for the change, the benefits it will bring, and the timeline of implementation. Address concerns and questions honestly to build trust and mitigate resistance.

- **Inclusivity and Collaboration**: Involve employees in the decision-making process whenever possible. Seek their input and feedback on the selection and implementation of new technology. This inclusivity empowers employees and makes them feel valued and invested in the transformation.

- **Addressing Concerns:** Acknowledge and address employee concerns proactively. Whether it's fear of job displacement, unfamiliarity with technology, or potential disruptions, providing accurate information and reassurances can alleviate anxieties.

- **Training and Support:** Comprehensive training is essential to ensure employees feel confident and competent in using the new technology. Offer training sessions that focus not only on technical skills but also on the benefits the technology brings to their daily tasks.

- **Demonstrating Quick Wins:** Showcase early successes and quick wins resulting from the adoption of new technology. Positive outcomes help build enthusiasm and demonstrate the tangible benefits of the change.
- **Empathy and Patience:** Recognize that change can be challenging for individuals. Demonstrate empathy and patience as employees adapt to the new technology. Offer support, resources, and a safe space for expressing concerns.
- **Change Agents:** Identify and empower change agents within the organization—individuals who are enthusiastic about the change and can influence their peers positively. These champions can motivate others and provide guidance.
- **Continuous Feedback:** Create avenues for employees to provide ongoing feedback about their experiences with the new technology. Listen to their insights and make adjustments based on their suggestions.
- **Celebrate Milestones:** Celebrate milestones and achievements during the implementation process. Recognize the hard work of employees and their successful adaptation to the changes.
- **Continuous Improvement:** Change is a dy-

namic process. Regularly assess the adoption of the technology, gather feedback, and refine your approach. Continuously seek opportunities to enhance the change management strategy.

- **Vision and Purpose:** Reinforce the overarching vision and purpose behind the adoption of smart technology. Help employees understand how their roles contribute to the organization's success and the larger impact on customer satisfaction and operational efficiency.

Change management requires a thoughtful and empathetic approach. Expert advice emphasizes the significance of leadership involvement, open communication, training, and addressing concerns to ensure a successful transition to smart technology adoption. By prioritizing the human aspect of change and fostering a collaborative and supportive environment, warehouses can empower their employees to embrace technology with enthusiasm and confidence, which ultimately drives the success of the transformation journey.

FOSTERING A CULTURE OF INNOVATION

- **Encourage Experimentation:** Create an environment where employees are encouraged to propose and test new ideas.
- **Reward Innovation:** Recognize and reward employees for contributing innovative ideas that improve warehouse operations.
- **Continuous Learning:** Invest in employee

development to keep them updated on emerging technologies and industry trends.

The challenges of adopting smart technology can be overcome with careful planning, strategic implementation, and a commitment to fostering an innovative culture. By addressing financial concerns, effectively integrating technology, and managing workforce transitions, warehouses can navigate the path to transformation. An organized implementation roadmap, coupled with open communication and change management strategies, ensures that the adoption of smart technology becomes a catalyst for positive change, efficiency gains, and sustained growth.

CHAPTER 9

Data Security and Privacy

Data security involves safeguarding digital data from unauthorized access, use, or theft. Privacy, on the other hand, pertains to the protection of individuals' personal information and ensures it is collected, processed, and stored in compliance with regulations and ethical considerations.

In the age of advanced warehouse management driven by technology, data has become a critical asset that powers efficient operations and personalized customer experiences. However, with the increasing reliance on data, ensuring its security and protecting customer privacy have become paramount concerns. This chapter delves into the complex landscape of data security and privacy within warehouse management and explores the challenges, strategies, and best practices for safeguarding sensitive information.

CHALLENGES IN WAREHOUSE DATA SECURITY AND PRIVACY

- **Vast Data Volume:** Warehouses generate and store massive amounts of data, including customer information, inventory details, and operational insights. Protecting this volume of data can be challenging.

- **Cybersecurity Threats**: The interconnected nature of technology exposes warehouses to various cyber threats, including hacking, data breaches, and ransomware attacks.

- **Regulatory Compliance**: Warehouses must adhere to data protection regulations, such as GDPR (General Data Protection Regulation) and CCPA (California Consumer Privacy Act), which mandate the proper handling of personal data.

STRATEGIES FOR DATA SECURITY AND PRIVACY

- **Robust Authentication:** Implement strong user authentication methods, such as multi-factor authentication, to ensure that only authorized personnel access sensitive data.

- **Data Encryption:** Encrypt data at rest and in transit to prevent unauthorized access even if data is compromised.

- **Regular Audits and Monitoring:** Regularly audit data access logs and monitor for suspicious activities to detect and respond to potential security breaches.

- **Employee Training:** Educate warehouse staff about data security best practices, including avoiding phishing scams and maintaining strong passwords.

- **Vendor Management**: If third-party vendors handle warehouse data, ensure they have robust security measures in place.

BEST PRACTICES FOR DATA PRIVACY

Revolutionizing your warehouse involves implementing cutting-edge technologies and innovative strategies to optimize operations and improve efficiency. However, amidst this digital transformation, it's crucial to prioritize data privacy to safeguard sensitive information and comply with relevant regulations. Here are some best practices for maintaining data privacy while revolutionizing your warehouse:

Data Mapping and Classification

Begin by conducting a comprehensive data inventory and mapping exercise. Identify all the types of data collected, processed, and stored within your warehouse ecosystem. Classify data based on its sensitivity, importance, and potential impact on individuals. This step forms the foundation for designing appropriate data protection measures.

Privacy by Design

Incorporate the concept of "privacy by design" into your warehouse's technological advancements. Ensure that data privacy considerations are embedded into the development and deployment of new systems, applications, and processes from the outset. This approach helps to prevent privacy issues from arising later in the project lifecycle.

Consent Management

If your warehouse collects personal data from employees, customers, or partners, obtain clear and informed consent for data processing activities. Implement mechanisms for obtaining and managing consent, and allow individuals to revoke their consent at any time. Communicate the purposes of data collection and usage to build trust.

Data Minimization

Collect and retain only the data necessary for your warehouse operations. Limit the amount of personal or sensitive information stored to minimize the risk associated with a data breach. Regularly review data holdings to ensure outdated or unnecessary data is securely disposed of.

Strong Access Controls

Implement strict access controls and user authentication mechanisms. Grant access rights based on the principle of least privilege and ensure that employees can only access the data and systems necessary for their roles. Regularly review and update access permissions as personnel roles change.

Encryption and Anonymization

Use encryption techniques to protect data both in transit and at rest. Anonymize or pseudonymize data whenever possible to reduce the risk of individual identification. This is especially important when sharing data for analysis or reporting purposes.

Regular Security Audits

Conduct regular security and privacy audits of your warehouse's systems and processes. Identify vulnerabilities, assess risks, and take corrective actions promptly. Regular audits help maintain compliance with regulations and industry standards.

Employee Training

Provide comprehensive training to all employees on data privacy principles and practices. Employees should understand their roles and responsibilities in maintaining data privacy, recognize potential threats, and know how to respond in case of a breach.

Vendor Management

If your warehouse relies on third-party vendors or partners for technology solutions, ensure they also adhere to robust data privacy practices. Evaluate their data handling processes, security measures, and compliance with relevant regulations before entering into partnerships.

Incident Response Plan

Develop a well-defined incident response plan that outlines steps to take in case of a data breach or privacy incident. This plan should include communication protocols, data breach containment procedures, and steps for notifying affected parties and regulatory authorities as required.

Continuous Monitoring and Improvement

Data privacy is an ongoing process. Continuously monitor your warehouse's data privacy practices, adapt to evolving threats and regulations, and make necessary improvements to your strategies and systems.

IMPLICATIONS OF DATA SECURITY AND PRIVACY VIOLATIONS

The significance of data security and privacy in warehouse operations cannot be overstated. Failure to adequately protect sensitive information can have far-reaching consequences that extend beyond financial implications. Understanding the potential implications of data security and privacy violations is essential for warehouses to prioritize robust cybersecurity measures and ensure compliance with regulations. Here's a detailed explanation of the implications:

Legal Penalties and Fines

Scenario: Data breaches or mishandling of customer data can lead to legal actions and regulatory fines.

Impact: Regulatory authorities, such as the Information Commissioner's Office (ICO) or the Federal Trade Commission (FTC), can impose substantial fines on warehouses that fail to comply with data protection regulations. These fines can amount to millions of dollars and severely impact the organization's finances.

Reputation Damage

Scenario: News of a data breach or privacy violation

spreads to the public and media.

Impact: Customer trust and brand reputation can suffer irreparable damage. Negative publicity can lead to decreased customer loyalty, reluctance to share personal information, and even a decline in sales. Rebuilding trust in the aftermath of a breach can be an uphill battle.

Loss of Customer Confidence

Scenario: Customers learn that their personal information was compromised in a data breach.

Impact: A breach can erode customers' confidence in the warehouse's ability to safeguard their data. Customers may choose to take their business elsewhere, which can affect customer retention rates and long-term profitability.

Litigation and Lawsuits

Scenario: Affected customers or stakeholders file lawsuits against the warehouse for negligence in protecting their data.

Impact: Lawsuits can result in substantial financial settlements and legal fees. Even if the warehouse successfully defends against legal claims, the process can be time-consuming and expensive.

Operational Disruption

Scenario: A data breach disrupts normal warehouse operations.

Impact: Responding to a breach requires allocating resources to investigate, contain, and mitigate the effects of the breach. This diversion of resources can disrupt regular operations and lead to efficiency losses and decreased productivity.

Customer Churn

Scenario: Customers concerned about data security decide to stop using the warehouse's services.

Impact: The loss of customers due to data security concerns can lead to reduced revenue and market share. Acquiring new customers to replace those lost due to a breach can be costly and challenging.

Decreased Investor Confidence

Scenario: Data breaches become public knowledge and lead to decreased investor confidence.

Impact: Stock prices may decline as a result of the negative publicity surrounding a breach. Investors may become wary of the organization's ability to manage risks, which could lead to decreased shareholder value.

Regulatory Scrutiny

Scenario: Regulatory authorities investigate the breach and the organization's data protection practices.

Impact: The warehouse may face ongoing regulatory scrutiny, audits, and increased oversight, which can divert resources away from core business activities.

Customer Communication

Scenario: The warehouse must notify affected customers about a data breach.

Impact: Communicating a breach requires careful messaging to prevent further panic and reassure customers. Mishandling the communication can exacerbate the damage to the warehouse's reputation.

Diminished Employee Morale

Scenario: A data breach affects employees' confidence in the organization's ability to protect their personal data.

Impact: Employees may feel disillusioned and demotivated and overall morale and productivity can drop.

In essence, the implications of data security and privacy violations extend beyond financial losses. They can irreparably harm an organization's reputation, customer trust, and market standing. To avoid these severe consequences, warehouses must prioritize cybersecurity measures, data protection best practices, and compliance with relevant regulations.

Data security and privacy are not just technical concerns; they are ethical imperatives. In the context of warehouse management, safeguarding data is essential to maintaining operational efficiency, customer trust, and regulatory compliance. By implementing robust security measures, following privacy best practices, and fostering a culture of data protection, warehouses can navigate the intricate landscape of data security and privacy while reaping the benefits of technology-driven innovation.

CHAPTER 10

Future Trends in Warehouse Management

As warehouse management continues to evolve, it's crucial to anticipate and prepare for the emerging technologies that will shape the industry's future. This chapter delves into the exciting possibilities on the horizon, such as 5G connectivity, blockchain, and augmented reality. It explores how these technologies are set to revolutionize the warehouse landscape and offer predictions on their impact. Furthermore, it emphasizes the importance of fostering a continuous learning mindset to stay ahead in a rapidly evolving field.

EXPLORING EMERGING TECHNOLOGIES

- **5G Connectivity:** The rollout of 5G networks promises ultra-fast, low-latency connectivity. This technology will enable real-time data transfer and support instant communication between devices, sensors, and systems within the warehouse.
- **Blockchain**: Blockchain technology offers transparent, tamper-proof data records. In the

warehouse context, it could enhance traceability, reduce fraud, and optimize supply chain transparency.

- **Augmented Reality (AR)**: AR overlays digital information onto the physical world. In warehouses, AR can guide workers in real time, streamline order picking, and provide visual instructions for complex tasks.

PREDICTIONS FOR FUTURE TRENDS

As warehouse management continues to evolve, several emerging technologies hold the potential to reshape the industry landscape in the coming years. These predictions offer insights into how these technologies might be integrated and how they could impact operations, efficiency, and customer experiences within warehouses. Here's a detailed exploration of the predictions for future trends in warehouse management:

Enhanced Connectivity Through 5G

Prediction: The widespread adoption of 5G connectivity will revolutionize communication within warehouses and across the supply chain.

Impact: Real-time data transfer will enable seamless communication between IoT devices, robots, and systems. This will lead to more accurate tracking, quicker decision-making, and reduced latency in remote operations.

Blockchain for Transparent Supply Chains

Prediction: Blockchain technology will become integral to maintaining transparent and secure supply chains.

Impact: By providing tamper-proof and immutable records of transactions, blockchain will enhance visibility, traceability, and authenticity across the supply chain. This will bolster trust among stakeholders and minimize fraud.

Augmented Reality for Enhanced Efficiency

Prediction: Augmented reality (AR) will transform warehouse operations through interactive visual overlays.

Impact: AR devices will guide workers in real time, which can optimize order picking, assembly, and maintenance tasks. This will reduce errors, speed up training, and make complex processes more intuitive.

Predictive Analytics for Demand Forecasting

Prediction: Predictive analytics will play a pivotal role in accurate demand forecasting.

Impact: By analyzing historical data and current trends, warehouses will be better equipped to anticipate fluctuations in demand. This will result in optimized inventory management, reduced overstocking, and improved order fulfillment.

Robotics and Automation in Fulfillment

Prediction: Robotics and automation will dominate warehouse fulfillment processes.

Impact: Autonomous robots will handle tasks, like picking, sorting, and packing, with higher precision and speed.

This will lead to reduced labor costs, increased accuracy, and shorter order processing times.

Sustainable Warehousing

Prediction: Warehouses will increasingly adopt sustainable practices to reduce environmental impact.

Impact: Solar panels, energy-efficient lighting, and eco-friendly packaging will become commonplace. Sustainable practices will not only reduce costs but also align warehouses with eco-conscious consumer preferences.

Voice and Natural Language Interfaces

Prediction: Voice technology and natural language interfaces will become essential for hands-free warehouse operations.

Impact: Workers will interact with systems and devices using voice commands, which can free up their hands and increase productivity. This will be particularly beneficial in environments where manual input is challenging.

Cloud-Based Solutions for Scalability

Prediction: Cloud-based warehouse management systems will become the norm.

Impact: Cloud solutions will provide scalability, flexibility, and remote accessibility. Warehouses will be able to quickly adjust to changing needs and seamlessly integrate new technologies.

Drone Delivery in Last-Mile Logistics

Prediction: Drones will play a significant role in last-mile logistics, particularly for small and urgent deliveries.

Impact: Drones will expedite deliveries, reduce transportation costs, and enable access to remote or hard-to-reach areas.

Continuous Learning and Upskilling

Prediction: The demand for upskilling and continuous learning will intensify as new technologies become prevalent.

Impact: Warehouse professionals will need to adapt their skill sets to work effectively with emerging technologies. Continuous learning will be critical for personal growth and career advancement.

These predictions highlight the transformative potential of emerging technologies in warehouse management. As 5G, blockchain, augmented reality, and other innovations become more integrated, warehouses have the opportunity to enhance operations, improve efficiency, and deliver exceptional customer experiences. Staying ahead of these trends through strategic planning, continuous learning, and proactive adoption of technology will be the key to success in the evolving landscape of warehouse management.

IMPORTANCE OF CONTINUOUS LEARNING

- **Staying Relevant in a Dynamic Environment:** Warehouse management is undergoing rapid transformation due to technological advancements and shifts in consumer behavior. Continuous learning ensures that professionals remain current with the latest trends, tools, and practices and enables them to contribute effectively to their organizations.

- **Adapting to New Technologies:** Technology plays a pivotal role in modern warehouse operations. Continuous learning empowers professionals to embrace and master new technologies, such as IoT, AI, and automation, which are driving efficiency and innovation in the field.
- **Enhancing Problem-Solving Skills:** Learning is not just about acquiring knowledge; it's about developing critical thinking and problem-solving abilities. Continuous learning exposes professionals to diverse perspectives and solutions and enables them to tackle challenges creatively and make informed decisions.
- **Maintaining Competitive Edge:** Professionals who prioritize continuous learning gain a competitive advantage. Their updated knowledge and skills set them apart and make them more valuable to their employers while positioning them for career advancement.
- **Responding to Industry Changes:** The warehouse industry is influenced by external factors, such as regulatory changes, market trends, and economic shifts. Continuous learning ensures professionals are equipped to respond to

these changes effectively and make strategic adjustments.

- **Personal Growth and Fulfillment:** Learning is a pathway to personal growth and fulfillment. Professionals who engage in continuous learning develop a sense of accomplishment, confidence, and intellectual curiosity that enriches their lives both inside and outside of work.

- **Embracing Innovation** A culture of continuous learning fosters a mindset of innovation. Professionals who are open to learning new concepts and approaches are more likely to experiment with novel ideas and drive positive change within their organizations.

- **Networking and Collaboration:** Learning provides opportunities to connect with industry peers, experts, and mentors. Networking and collaborating with others in the field lead to the exchange of knowledge, best practices, and insights that can be applied to improve warehouse operations.

- **Adapting to Customer Expectations:** Customer expectations are evolving rapidly and are driven by the convenience and personalization they experience in other industries. Continuous learning enables professionals to understand these changing expectations and tailor warehouse strategies to meet them.

- **Fostering Resilience:** Learning is a tool for

building resilience. Professionals who actively engage in learning are better equipped to navigate challenges, setbacks, and uncertainties with a positive and adaptable mindset.

The future of warehouse management is bright and technology-driven. 5G connectivity, blockchain, and augmented reality are just a few of the emerging technologies set to reshape the industry. Embracing these trends requires a commitment to continuous learning and an open mindset. Warehouse professionals who stay informed, adapt to change, and proactively integrate new technologies into their operations will be at the forefront of innovation, which will set the stage for a dynamic and prosperous future.

CONCLUSION

In conclusion, embarking on the journey to revolutionize your warehouse through the embrace of smart technology is not just a strategic choice—it's a transformative leap toward operational excellence and competitive advantage. The convergence of cutting-edge technologies, such as the Internet of Things (IoT), Artificial Intelligence (AI), and automation, promises to reshape the way warehouses function and businesses operate.

By adopting smart technology, your warehouse stands to reap numerous benefits, including everything from enhanced efficiency and streamlined processes to improved accuracy and real-time visibility. The seamless integration of digital solutions enables you to optimize inventory management, expedite order fulfillment, and deliver an unparalleled customer experience. Moreover, the reduction in human error, increased safety measures, and efficient space utilization contribute to a workplace that is not only productive but also conducive to innovation.

The transformation extends beyond the warehouse walls—it redefines how your business interacts with the supply chain ecosystem. Data-driven insights enable informed decision-making, while predictive analytics refine inventory strategies and demand forecasting. This, in turn, fosters agility in adapting to market shifts and customer preferences.

As you embrace smart technology, it's vital to remember that this evolution is not a mere trend but a pivotal shift that holds the potential to shape the future of warehousing and commerce. Embracing digital transformation positions your business at the forefront of innovation and empowers you to navigate a dynamic landscape and seize new opportunities with confidence.

In embracing the smart technology that transforms your business, you're not only modernizing operations; you're catalyzing growth, cultivating efficiency, and embracing a future where your warehouse is not just a functional space but a strategic asset that propels your business toward success in an increasingly competitive world. The journey is challenging yet rewarding, and it places your business firmly on the path to excellence and sustainability. So, embark on this transformational voyage and empower your warehouse to become a beacon of innovation and progress in the realm of commerce.

ABOUT THE AUTHOR

Somil Nishar is an accomplished professional in the realm of automation engineering, renowned for his extensive practical experience and academic prowess. With a distinguished background in the field, Somil has dedicated himself to the pursuit of excellence, innovation, and transformative solutions in automation.

Somil's academic journey is highlighted by a Master of Science in Engineering specialized in Mechatronics, Robotics, and Automation Engineering from Colorado State University Pueblo. This academic foundation has empowered him with an in-depth understanding of the theoretical aspects that underpin modern automation technologics. Additionally, his Master's degree in Project Management from the University of the Cumberland reflects his commitment to effective project execution, strategic planning, and seamless communication.

Somil's expertise is not limited to technical implementations; he also excels in disseminating knowledge and insights. He is known for his ability to present complex concepts in a clear and accessible manner, making him a sought-after educator and thought leader in the field.